The AZTECS

MYTHS of the WORLD

THE AZTECS

VIRGINIA SCHOMP

MARSHALL CAVENDISH · BENCHMARK
NEW YORK

$\backsim$ *For Fred, Marlene, Freddy, and Ashley Schmidt* $\backsim$

The author would like to thank Kay Almere Read, Professor of History of Religions,
Religious Studies Department, DePaul University, Chicago,
for her valuable comments and careful reading of the manuscript.

Benchmark Books Marshall Cavendish 99 White Plains Road Tarrytown, New York 10591
www.marshallcavendish.com Text copyright © 2009 by Marshall Cavendish Corporation All rights reserved.
No part of this book may be reproduced or utilized in any form or by any means electronic or mechanical,
including photocopying, recording, or by any information storage and retrieval system, without permission
from the copyright holders. All Internet sites were available and accurate when this book was sent to press.
LIBRARY OF CONGRESS CATALOGING-IN-PUBLICATION DATA Schomp, Virginia. The Aztecs / by Virginia Schomp. p.
cm. — (Myths of the world) Summary: "A retelling of several key Aztec myths, with background information describing the history, geography, belief systems, and customs of the Aztecs"—Provided by publisher.
Includes bibliographical references and index. ISBN 978-0-7614-3096-4 1. Aztecs—Juvenile literature. I.
Title. F1219.73.S36 2009 972—dc22 2008007082

EDITOR: Joyce Stanton   ART DIRECTOR: Anahid Hamparian
PUBLISHER: Michelle Bisson   SERIES DESIGNER: Michael Nelson

Images provided by Rose Corbett Gordon, Art Editor, of Mystic CT, from the following sources: Cover: The
Art Archive/Government Palace Tiaxcala Mexico/Gianni Dagli Orti Back cover: The British Museum/HIP/
The Image Works Pages 1, 7, 37, 43, 47, 73: Werner Forman/Art Resource, NY; pages 2-3, 67, 68, 75, 88 top:
Gianni Dagli Orti/Corbis; page 6: Kenneth Garrett Photographer; page 8: John Bigelow Taylor/Art Resource,
NY; pages 9, 27, 32-33, 89 top: The Art Archive/Mexican National Library/Mireille Vautier; pages 10-11, 18
bottom, 48, 50, 52, 89 bottom: © 2008 Banco de México Diego Rivera & Frida Kahlo Museums Trust. Av.
Cinco de Mayo No. 2, Col. Centro, Del. Cuauhtémoc 06059, México, D.F., The Art Archive/National Palace
Mexico City/Gianni Dagli Orti; page 12: The Art Archive/Queretaro Museum Mexico/Gianni Dagli Orti; page
14: Museo Nacional de Antropologia, Mexico City, Mexico/Sean Sprague/Mexicolore/Bridgeman Art Library;
page 16: The Art Archive/National Museum of Art Mexico/Gianni Dagli Orti; page 18 top: Nicolas
Sapieha/Art Resource, NY; page 19: AAAC/Topham/The Image Works; pages 20, 49: Bettmann/Corbis; pages
22, 62, 85: Bildarchiv Preussischer Kulturbesitz/Art Resource, NY; pages 24, 87: The Art Archive/National
Anthropological Museum; Mexico/Gianni Dagli Orti; pages 26, 38, 54, 55, 81:Werner Forman/Topham/The
Image Works; page 28: British Museum/Art Resource, NY; pages 30, 44, 46: The Art Archive/Museo Ciudad
Mexico/Gianni Dagli Orti; pages 31, 80: The Art Archive/Biblioteca Nacional Madrid/Gianni Dagli Orti;
pages 34, 36, 88 bottom: The Art Archive/Antochiw Collection Mexico/Mireille Vautier; page 37: Werner
Forman/Art Resource, NY; page 40: The Art Archive/Templo Mayor Library Mexico/Gianni Dagli Orti; page
42: The Art Archive/National Archives Mexico/Mireille Vautier; page 53: The LuEsther T. Mertz Library,
NYBG/Art Resource, NY; page 56: Archives Charmet/Bridgeman Art Library; page 57: The Art
Archive/Museo de America Madrid/Gianni Dagli Orti; pages 58, 60: Museo Nacional de Antropologia,
Mexico City, Mexico, Jean-Pierre Courau/The Bridgeman Art Library International; page 61: Gilles
Mermet/Art Resource, NY; page 63: Museo del Templo Mayor, Mexico City, Mexico/Bildarchiv
Steffens/Bridgeman Art Library; pages 64, 66: Schalkwijk/Art Resource, NY; page 69: Michel Zabé/Art
Resource, NY; pages 71, 76, 78, 82, 84: The Granger Collection, NY; page 72: Stapleton Collection/Corbis;
page 83: Bridgeman-Giraudon/Art Resource, NY; page 86: Michel Zabé/Art Resource, NY.

Printed in Malaysia
135642

Front cover: The beloved god Quetzalcoatl gives the Aztecs the gift of maize, or corn.
Half-title page: Tezcatlipoca, god of the night and darkness, lost his foot in a battle with a fearsome monster.
Title page: According to mythology, the god Huitzilopochtli sent an eagle to show the Aztecs where to build
their empire.
Back cover: This turquoise mosaic of a two-headed serpent may have been worn as an ornament during
religious ceremonies.

CONTENTS

THE MAGIC *of* MYTHS

EVERY ANCIENT CULTURE HAD ITS MYTHS. These timeless tales of gods and heroes give us a window into the beliefs, values, and practices of people who lived long ago. They can make us think about the BIG QUESTIONS that have confronted humankind down through the ages: questions about human nature, the meaning of life, and what happens after death. On top of all that, myths are simply great stories that are lots of fun to read.

What makes a story a myth? Unlike a narrative written by a particular author, a myth is a traditional story that has been handed down from generation to generation, first orally and later in written form. Nearly all myths tell the deeds of gods, goddesses, and other divine beings. These age-old tales were once widely accepted as true and sacred. Their primary purpose was to explain the mysteries of life and the origins of a society's customs, institutions, and religious rituals.

It is sometimes hard to tell the difference between a myth and a heroic legend. Both myths and legends are traditional stories that may include extraordinary elements such as gods, spirits, magic, and monsters. Both may be partly based on real events in the distant past. However, the main characters in legends are usually mortals rather than divine beings. Another key difference is that legends are basically exciting action stories, while myths almost always express deeper meanings or truths.

Above: The Aztecs believed that the sun traveled through the underworld each night in the form of a fierce jaguar.

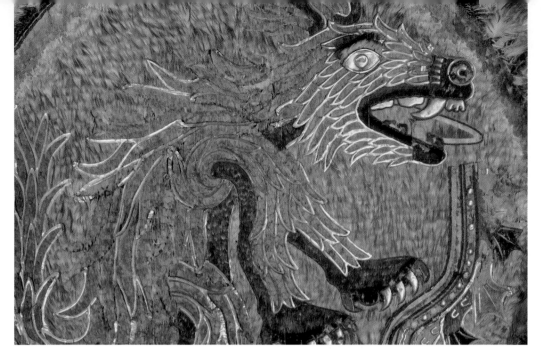

Mythology (the whole collection of myths belonging to a society) played an important role in ancient cultures. In very early times, people created myths to explain the awe-inspiring, uncontrollable forces of nature, such as thunder, lightning, darkness, drought, and death. Even after science began to develop more rational explanations for these mysteries, myths continued to provide comforting answers to the many questions that could never be fully resolved. People of nearly all cultures have asked the same basic questions about the world around them. That is why myths from different times and places can be surprisingly similar. For example, the people of almost every ancient culture told stories about the creation of the world, the origins of gods and humans, the changing of the seasons, and the afterlife.

Mythology served ancient cultures as instruction, inspiration, and entertainment. It offered a way for the people of a society to express their fundamental beliefs and values and pass them down to future generations. It helped preserve memories of their civilization's past glories and held up examples of ideal human qualities and conduct. Finally, these imaginative stories provided enjoyment to countless listeners and readers in ancient times, just as they do today.

Above: This mythical water beast preyed on people traveling beside lakes and rivers.

The MYTHS OF THE WORLD series explores the mythology of some of history's greatest civilizations. Each book opens with a brief look at the culture that created the myths, including its geographical setting, political history, government, society, and religious beliefs. Next comes the fun part: the stories themselves. We based our retellings of the myths selected for these books on a variety of traditional sources. The new versions are fun and easy to read. At the same time, we have strived to remain true to the spirit of the ancient tales, preserving their magic, their mystery, and the special ways of speech and avenues of thought that made each culture unique.

As you read the myths, you will come across sidebars, or text boxes, highlighting topics related to each story's characters or themes. The sidebars in *The Aztecs* include excerpts from a variety of early chronicles and poems. The sources for these excerpts are noted on page 93. You will find lots of other useful material at the back of the book as well, including information on Aztec writing and texts, a glossary of difficult terms, suggestions for further reading, and more. Finally, the stories are illustrated with both ancient and modern paintings, sculptures, and other works of art inspired by mythology. These images can help us better understand the spirit of the myths and the way a society's traditional tales have influenced other cultures through the ages.

Now it is time to begin our adventures with the Aztecs. We hope that you will enjoy this journey to a land where mysterious gods and goddesses govern the course of human lives, the destiny of empires, and the fate of the universe itself. Most of all, we hope that the sampling of stories and art in this book will inspire you to further explorations of the magical world of mythology.

An Aztec warrior dressed as an eagle, symbol of military skill and courage

A NOTE ON PRONUNCIATIONS

The names of the Aztec gods and goddesses are hard to spell and even harder to pronounce. The following guidelines may help. When in doubt, do what we do: just say the names any way that makes it easy for you to read and enjoy these wonderful old stories!

Vowels
a sounds like *ah*

e sounds like *ay*

i sounds like *ee*

o sounds like *oh*

Consonants
c (before e or i) sounds like *s*

c (before a or o) sounds like *k*

cu sounds like *kw*

hu and uh sound like *w*

qu (before a) sounds like *kw*

qu (before e or i) sounds like *k*

When tl appears at the end of a word, the l is silent.

x sounds like *sh*

z sounds like *s*

Above: Xochipilli (pronounced shoh-chee-PEE-lee) was an Aztec god of flowers and souls.

Part 1
MEET *the* AZTECS

The LAND BETWEEN *the* WATERS

ABOUT EIGHT HUNDRED YEARS AGO, A WANDERING tribe called the Mexica migrated down from the north to the region known today as the Valley of Mexico. They found a large plateau surrounded by even higher hills and mountains. Five shallow lakes covered much of this fertile blue-green highland. The Mexica named their new home Anahuac, or the "Land between the Waters." Within a few decades, they would transform their tiny village in Anahuac into the center of a mighty empire. Today we call the people of that empire Aztecs, for Aztlan, their mythical homeland to the north.

The Aztecs lived in a world that was unstable and unpredictable. The Valley of Mexico was ringed by volcanoes that could erupt at any moment, spewing ash, lava, and glowing rocks. Frequent earthquakes shook the ground. The spring rains brought both life-giving waters and devastating floods. Some years the rains failed, and crops withered in

Opposite: A painting by Mexican artist Joaquin Ramirez depicts the Mexica's arrival in the Valley of Mexico.

Previous page: Farmers sell several varieties of corn at a busy Aztec marketplace.

The Aztecs' island capital, Tenochtitlán, was vulnerable to floods and earthquakes.

the fields. Thousands of men, women, and children could starve when the harvest was lost to drought or other natural disasters such as locusts or killing frosts.

Aztec mythology reflected the wonders and dangers of this changeable environment. In "The Five Suns" on page 35, we will learn how the gods created a series of worlds, then destroyed them with catastrophes including a flood and a rain of fire. We will also see how fire and death brought the light of the sun to the present world.

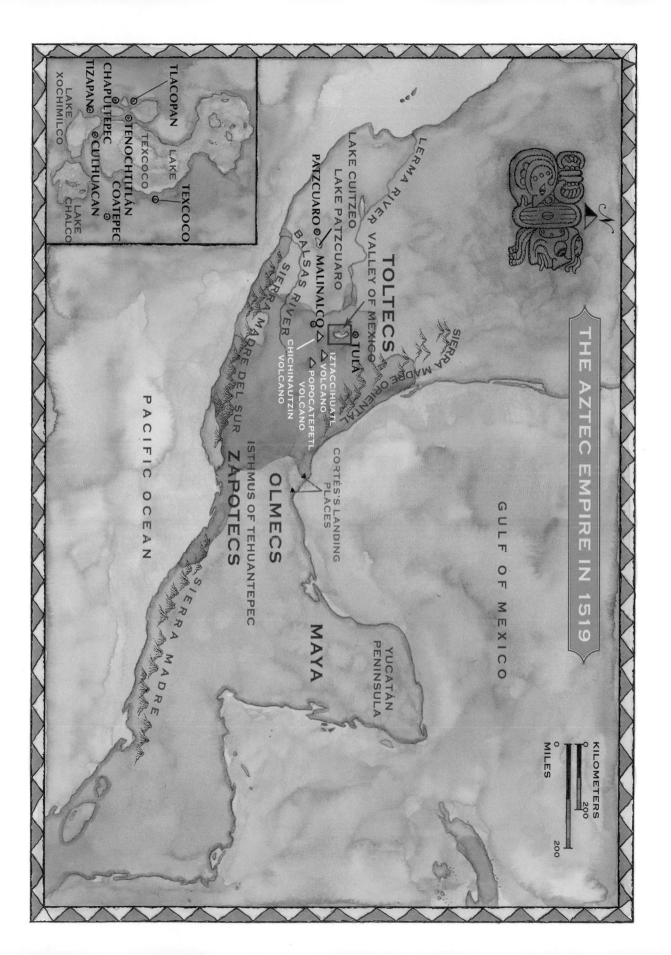

THE AZTEC EMPIRE IN 1519

KILOMETERS
0   200
MILES
0   200

TLACOPAN
LAKE XOCHIMILCO
CHAPULTEPEC
TIZAPAN
TENOCHTITLÁN
COATEPEC
CUITHUACAN
LAKE TEXCOCO
TEXCOCO
LAKE CHALCO
TEXCOCO

LERMA RIVER
VALLEY OF MEXICO
LAKE CUITZEO
LAKE PÁTZCUARO
PÁTZCUARO
TOLTECS
MALINALCO
TULA
IZTACCÍHUATL VOLCANO
POPOCATEPETL VOLCANO
CHICHINAUTZIN VOLCANO
SIERRA MADRE ORIENTAL
CORTÉS'S LANDING PLACES
GULF OF MEXICO

SIERRA MADRE DEL SUR
BALSAS RIVER
SIERRA MADRE
OLMECS
ZAPOTECS
ISTHMUS OF TEHUANTEPEC

PACIFIC OCEAN
SIERRA MADRE

MAYA
YUCATÁN PENINSULA

N

A MIGHTY EMPIRE

*T*HE VALLEY OF MEXICO IS LOCATED IN MESOAMERICA, an area that includes present-day Mexico, Guatemala, Belize, and other parts of Central America. The Aztecs were the last of several great civilizations to emerge in this region. The Olmecs, the area's first advanced culture, dated all the way back to the twelfth century BCE. Other important Mesoamerican civilizations included the Zapotecs, Toltecs, and Maya.

Wandering groups of Mexica first arrived in the Valley of Mexico around the middle of the thirteenth century CE. By that time, most of the earlier Mesoamerican cultures had declined. A number of small, warring city-states inhabited the Land between the Waters. The Mexica roamed from place to place, seeking a home among all these hostile peoples. They finally settled on the shores of wide, shallow Lake Texcoco.

Opposite: According to mythology, the Aztecs' ancestors endured a long and difficult journey before arriving in the Valley of Mexico.

Aztec farmers used mud and wooden stakes to create thousands of *chinampa* fields.

The Mexica proved to be capable farmers. They planted corn and other crops in *chinampas*, narrow strips of farmland created by piling up mud in the shallow lake beds. They also won acclaim as warriors, fighting in the armies of their stronger neighbors. In 1325 they established their own city on a swampy island in the middle of Lake Texcoco. They named their new capital Tenochtitlán (tay-notch-teet-LAHN), or "Place of the Prickly Pear Cactus."

This imaginative scene from an open-air market overlooking Tenochtitlán is part of a mural by the famous Mexican artist Diego Rivera.

Over the next century, the Mexica built a strong, disciplined military and expanded their territories. Around 1428 they were powerful enough to form an alliance with two neighboring city-states, Texcoco and Tlacopan. That Triple Alliance, with the Mexica as the dominant member, forged the mighty Aztec Empire. The fierce Aztec armies conquered a vast realm stretching across Mesoamerica, from the Pacific Ocean to the Gulf of Mexico. The heart of the realm was Tenochtitlán. This magnificent capital became one of the largest and most sophisticated cities in the world, reaching an estimated population between 250,000 and 300,000.

The Spanish soldier and adventurer Hernán Cortés led the armies that conquered the Aztec Empire.

The Aztec Empire lasted less than one hundred years. In 1519 Spanish soldiers led by Hernán Cortés sailed to Mexico in search of land and treasure. Cortés formed alliances with the Aztecs' enemies. Within two years, the Spaniards and their native allies had toppled the last Aztec emperor and demolished Tenochtitlán. Aztec accounts of the Spanish Conquest blamed the swift and violent end of their great civilization on spiritual forces. "Tales of the Conquest" on page 77 retells that blending of history and ancient myths.

A variety of systems of dating have been used by different cultures throughout history. Many historians now prefer to use BCE (Before Common Era) and CE (Common Era) instead of BC (Before Christ) and AD (Anno Domini), out of respect for the diversity of the world's peoples.

The SOCIAL PYRAMID

AZTEC SOCIETY WAS ORGANIZED LIKE A PYRAMID. At the base was a vast body of *macehualtin* (mah-say-WAL-teen), or commoners. The commoners included farmers, fishermen, laborers, craftsmen, and merchants. These hardworking people paid taxes in the form of products. They also were required to labor on public projects such as roads, bridges, and temples and to serve as soldiers in the Aztec army. The children of commoners went to local schools, where they were taught basic occupational skills, the elements of warfare, and good citizenship.

Some *macehualtin* rose above their fellow commoners to join the narrow middle class. Promising young students were prepared for careers in the priesthood. Brave warriors rose through the military ranks. Gifted painters, goldsmiths, feather workers, and other artisans created luxury goods for the upper classes, while clever sellers became rich city merchants. The most honored merchants were the *pochteca*

Opposite:
A farmer carrying a wooden digging stick plants the seeds for a fruit tree.

The emperor's finery included a richly decorated cloak and an elegant feathered fan.

(poach-TEK-ah), or "traders," who traveled to distant lands to bring back coveted goods such as gold and jaguar skins.

At the peak of Aztec society was a small but powerful group of nobles. These high-born individuals included priests, military leaders, and government officials. Nobles had many special privileges, including the right to own land. The wealthiest members of this class lived in great luxury, enjoying the finest homes, food, clothing, and jewels. The children of nobles attended special schools, where priests instructed them in the history and traditions of their elders and the skills of governing.

The noblest of all nobles was the emperor, or *huey tlatoani* (way tlah-toe-AH-nee). The *tlatoani* was the head of the government, chief priest, and commander in chief of the army. He was responsible for making sure the gods were properly worshipped and for expanding the empire through war. This exalted ruler was elected by a small group of high-ranking nobles, but the Aztecs believed that he was really appointed by the gods.

Aztec society was dominated by men. Women were generally expected to marry and dedicate themselves to their roles as wives and mothers. Although the man was the unquestioned head of the household, wives often enjoyed considerable respect and influence within their own homes. A woman who gave birth was honored as a "valiant warrior." Women also might fight fiercely to defend their homes and families in times of war.

Aztec mythology reflected these vigorous roles. In "Quetzalcoatl Visits the Underworld" on page 45, we will meet the goddess Cihuacoatl, who helped create the people of the present world. "The Birth of Huitzilopochtli" on page 59 introduces us to two goddesses often associated with war and sacrifice, Coatlicue and her daughter Coyolxauhqui.

The SACRED WORLD

THE AZTECS BELIEVED THAT EVERYTHING IN THE WORLD, from the cry of a newborn infant to the vast ocean, was alive with sacred powers. In some cases those powers took on a humanlike form. The Aztec word for these mysterious spirits was *teotl* (TAY-aht). We might call them gods and goddesses.

The list of Aztec gods and goddesses was nearly endless. A few of these divine beings came to Mexico with the Mexica people. Most were adopted from the religions of the Mesoamerican peoples that the Aztecs conquered. A single god might have several different names and functions and might be represented in several forms. Adding to the confusion, the deities often overlapped in their areas of responsibility. For example, a number of different *teotl* were associated with the growing of corn.

Opposite: Xipe Totec was a complex god associated with new growth and the spring, as well as sacrifice and torture.

Three gods dominated the Aztec religion:

TEZCATLIPOCA, whose name means "Lord of the Smoking Mirror," was all-knowing, all-powerful, and ever-present. He was often associated with the night and darkness. Tezcatlipoca used his magical black mirror to see into the future and search out the secrets in people's hearts.

QUETZALCOATL, the "Plumed Serpent," created human beings and gave them many valuable gifts, including agriculture, corn, and the calendar. This beloved god was associated with the morning star, the wind, and priestly wisdom. He was often represented as a serpent covered with the bright green feathers of the quetzal bird.

This stone sculpture shows Quetzalcoatl carrying a load of corncobs on his back.

HUITZILOPOCHTLI was a fierce god of war and the sun. He led the Mexica people to their island home of Tenochtitlán. His name, which means "Hummingbird on the Left" (or "from the South"), reflects his connection with war and death. The Aztecs believed that hummingbirds were the souls of dead warriors, returning from the paradise of the sun in the South.

Along with these three gods, the Aztecs worshipped a bewildering variety of other deities. There were gods of the trees, mountains, fire, music, dancing, feasting, hunting, gambling, love, beauty, and nearly

A stream flows from the skirts of Chalchiuhtlicue, goddess of water.

every other aspect of existence. Many divine beings were involved with fertility, water, and rain, reflecting the importance of farming in Aztec life. The chief rain god was Tlaloc, or "He Who Makes Things Grow." His sister-wife Chalchiuhtlicue ("She of the Jade Skirt") watched over rivers, lakes, and streams. Another important agricultural deity was Xipe Totec. Like the other Aztec deities, Xipe Totec had several different aspects. As the god of springtime, he watched over seeds, planting, and the growing crops. In his darker forms, he could bring scabs, blindness, and dreadful diseases.

The AZTEC GODS and GODDESSES

The Aztecs worshipped thousands of different gods and goddesses. Here are some of the most important deities featured in this book, with their special areas of responsibility.

QUETZALCOATL
God of the morning star, the wind, and the priesthood

TEZCATLIPOCA
God of the night and darkness

HUITZILOPOCHTLI
God of war and the sun; patron god of the Aztecs

OMETEOTL
Father and mother of the gods

TLALOC
God of the rain and agricultural fertility

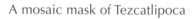

A mosaic mask of Tezcatlipoca

CHALCHIUHTLICUE
Goddess of lakes, rivers, streams, and mountains; wife of Tlaloc

XIPE TOTEC
God of new growth and the spring

MICTLANTECUHTLI
God of the dead

MICTLANCIHUATL
Goddess of the dead; wife of Mictlantecuhtli

SERVANTS *of the* GODS

RELIGION WAS AN IMPORTANT PART OF DAILY LIFE for every Aztec man, woman, and child. The sacred forces that inhabited every part of the world could bring rain or drought, victory or defeat, order or chaos. The world would survive only if the people did everything possible to secure the blessings of these powerful, unpredictable beings.

Every Aztec home had a small shrine, where the family often gathered to worship the gods and ask for their continued protection. People also performed prayers and rituals as they went about their daily routines. Farmers made offerings to the gods of the rain, sun, earth, and corn. Fishermen appealed to the deities of the waters. Midwives called on the goddesses of birth to watch over women in labor and newborn infants. Everyone took part in the endless round of public festivals that honored the gods through rituals, poetry, plays, music, and dancing.

The Templo Mayor ("Great Temple") in Tenochtitlán was an inspiring setting for sacred rituals.

Priests and priestesses cared for the sacred images of the gods, which were housed in shrines atop pyramid-shaped temples. They also performed sacred ceremonies that helped preserve the balance and order of the universe. These rituals centered around offerings to the gods, which might include gifts of plants, sacrificial animals, gold, or precious gems. The most precious gift of all was human blood.

All worshippers, young and old, offered their blood to the gods by puncturing their earlobes, tongues, and other parts of the body. Priests cut themselves so often that their earlobes became permanently shredded. The Aztecs also sacrificed as many as 20,000 men, women, and children a year during spectacular religious ceremonies. Most sacrificial victims were prisoners captured in war. Others might be slaves or free individuals chosen for their beauty or other special qualities. Some victims were unwilling participants, while others went proudly to their deaths.

Today we might wonder how the people of such an advanced culture could practice human sacrifice. The answer may be found in Aztec mythology. According to the ancient stories, the gods sacrificed

The Aztecs believed that the blood of sacrificial victims fed the gods and ensured the survival of the world.

their blood to create humans and set the sun moving in the sky. In return for these great gifts, humans were expected to provide the gods with nourishment in the form of human blood. Without regular blood sacrifices, the sun might stop rising. The waters might dry up, and the earth might lose its fertility. In the stories that follow, we will learn how the Aztecs came to see themselves as a people divinely chosen to nourish the gods and sustain the very existence of the world.

Part 2

TIMELESS TALES *of* THE AZTECS

THE ORIGINS *of* *the* WORLD

The Five Suns

ACCORDING TO AZTEC MYTHOLOGY, A SERIES OF FOUR worlds existed before the present age. Each of these four worlds, which the Aztecs called Suns, was ruled by a different god or goddess. During each age, a different race of beings populated the earth. In time, each world was destroyed, and the inhabitants were either wiped out or transformed into some other form of life. Finally, the gods created the Fifth Sun, the world we inhabit today.

The ancient myth of the Five Suns introduces us to several important Aztec deities. Ometeotl was the source of all existence. This great creator god had a dual (double) nature, combining both male and female forms within one mysterious being. He/she had four sons: Quetzalcoatl, the beloved god associated with the morning star; Tezcatlipoca, who represented the night and darkness; Xipe Totec, god of springtime; and Huitzilopochtli, patron god of the Aztecs. Other key players in the creation story include the rain god Tlaloc and his sister-wife Chalchiuhtlicue,

Opposite: Quetzalcoatl is adorned with feathers and armed with his serpent-shaped spear-thrower. The god's name reflects his different characteristics: *quetzal* means "feathered" or "plumed" and *coatl* means "serpent."

Previous page: Tonatiuh, god of the sun, towers over a priest who is honoring him with the burning of incense.

goddess of the waters. The conflicts and cooperation among all these deities resulted in both the creation and destruction of the worlds.

The Aztecs recorded their creation story and other myths in texts known as codices. The codices were books consisting mainly of pictographs, or word pictures, painted on long, folded scrolls of paper made from bark or deerskin. After the conquest of Mexico, the Spaniards burned most of these sacred texts in an effort to stamp out the Aztec religion. At the same time, a few Spanish missionaries collected and recorded many ancient songs and stories that had been passed down orally for generations. Aztec writers also created new codices about their vanishing traditions. Modern-day scholars have pieced together the Aztec creation myth with the help of these post-Conquest texts.

CAST *of* CHARACTERS

Ometeotl (oh-may-TAY-oat) Father and mother of the gods

Xipe Totec (SHEE-pee TOE-tek) God of new growth and the spring

Tezcatlipoca (tez-kaht-lee-PO-kah) God of the night and darkness

Quetzalcoatl (ket-sal-KO-waht) God of the morning star

Huitzilopochtli (weet-see-lo-POACH-tlee) God of war and the sun; patron god of the Aztecs

Tlaloc (TLAH-lok) God of rain

Chalchiuhtlicue (chal-chee-oot-LEE-kway) Goddess of lakes, rivers, streams, and mountains

Tecuciztecatl (tay-kwah-seez-TAY-kaht) God of snails and the moon

Nanahuatzin (nah-nah-WAHT-seen) God of skin diseases

Tonatiuh (toe-nah-TEE-wah) God of the sun

The First Four Ages

IN ANCIENT TIMES there was only one god, whose name was Ometeotl. This mysterious being was both male and female. He was Ometecuhtli, Lord of Duality. She was Omecihuatl, Lady of Duality. He/she dwelt in one body, in a universe bathed in darkness.

Ometeotl gave birth to four children. The oldest was called Xipe Totec. The second and biggest son was Tezcatlipoca. The third brother was Quetzalcoatl. The fourth and smallest brother was Huitzilopochtli.

Ometeotl was the source of all creation. This stone sculpture shows the god as a wise old man.

Together the four brothers created the First Sun. They made the heavens and earth and underworld. They made time itself, creating the days and dividing them into months. They created a race of primitive giants, who ate nothing but acorns but were strong enough to pull up trees with their bare hands. The four gods also created Tlaloc and his sister-wife Chalchiuhtlicue, so that the giants would have someone to ask for water. Then Tezcatlipoca turned himself into the sun so that there would be light on the earth.

The First Sun lasted 676 years. Then Quetzalcoatl took a club and knocked his brother out of the sky. The mighty god fell into the sea. When he rose from the water, he was so angry that he turned into a jaguar and devoured all the giants on earth.

After that, Quetzalcoatl became the sun. He created a new race of people, who had nothing to eat but pine nuts. The Second Sun lasted 364 years. Then Tezcatlipoca took revenge on his brother. He raised a great blast of wind that swept the sun from the sky. The fierce wind blew away all the trees and houses. It carried off all the people, except for a few

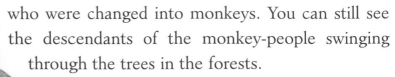

who were changed into monkeys. You can still see the descendants of the monkey-people swinging through the trees in the forests.

Next Tlaloc, god of rain, became the sun. The people of this age ate a seed like wheat, which sprouts in the water. The Third Sun lasted 312 years. Then Quetzalcoatl sent a rain of fire. The sun went up in flames, and the trees and houses were consumed by red-hot lava. All the people burned up, except for a few who turned into birds and flew above the molten earth until it cooled and hardened.

Now Tlaloc's wife, Chalchiuhtlicue, became the sun. In this age the people of the earth lived on a wild seed that was the ancestor of true corn.

The people who survived the destruction of the Second Sun were turned into monkeys.

The Fourth Sun lasted 676 years. Then it rained so long and so hard that the floodwaters rose over the tops of the mountains. All the people were turned into fishes. The sky itself came falling down, washing the sun along with it.

At last the rains stopped. For 52 years the earth lay still, dark, and silent under its blanket of water. Then the four sons of Ometeotl decided to create a space where life could begin again. They made four roads to the center of the earth. They crawled under the edges of the fallen sky, each in a separate quarter. Working together, they raised up the sky-waters.

To keep the sky from falling again, Quetzalcoatl and Tezcatlipoca turned themselves into two enormous trees. The Quetzalcoatl tree glinted with the emerald green feathers of the quetzal bird. The

Tezcatlipoca tree glowed with smoky black mirrors. To this day those two mighty trees still support the sky above the earth.

In appreciation of their great deed, Ometeotl made Quetzalcoatl and Tezcatlipoca masters of the sky and stars. Leaving their trees in place, the two gods walked through the heavens. The white road they traveled on can still be seen in the night sky. Today we call it the Milky Way.

The Fifth Sun

After the creation of the fifth world, the gods gathered together in the heavens. "The earth remains in darkness," they said. "Who among us will take it upon himself to become the new sun?"

Tecuciztecatl, the fine and wealthy lord of snails, stepped forward. "O gods, I shall be the one!" he said proudly.

Again the gods spoke. "One is not enough for this important task. Who will be the other one? Who will help bring the dawn?"

This time no one came forward. All the gods were too afraid. They knew that whoever volunteered must sacrifice himself in the fire so that the sun could be born again.

As the gods worried and wondered what to do, Nanahuatzin stood watching. This humble god was small, weak, and misshapen. His skin was covered with ugly sores. He did not dare present himself in the same company as strong, handsome Tecuciztecatl. But when no one else volunteered, the gods turned to him at last. "You! You shall be the one to give light, Nanahuatzin!"

The little god's heart leaped with gladness. "I accept!" he cried quickly. "O gods, you have honored me!"

So the two volunteers prepared themselves to celebrate the sacred rituals. For four days they purified their bodies by fasting. They made

The EARTH MONSTER

According to one version of the Aztec creation story, Quetzalcoatl and Tezcatlipoca worked together to re-create the earth after the destruction of the Fourth Sun. Raw materials for their creation came from the earth goddess Tlaltecuhtli. This monster had hungry mouths all over her body. Quetzalcoatl and Tezcatlipoca captured her, tore her in two, and used the halves to create the sky and earth. The Aztecs believed that earthquakes were complaints from the mutilated goddess. Only flesh and blood could soothe her hunger and ensure her continued blessings.

The following retelling of this ancient story comes from the *Histoyre du Mechique*, a French translation of a sixteenth-century Spanish text on Aztec mythology.

[Quetzalcoatl and Tezcatlipoca] changed themselves into two large snakes, of which one seized the goddess from the right hand to the left foot, the other from the left hand to the right foot, and they pulled so much that they broke her in half, and from the half towards the shoulders they made the earth and carried off the other half to heaven. . . .

After this deed, in order to recompense [repay] the goddess of the earth for the damage that the two gods had done to her, all the gods came down to console her, and ordered that from her would come all the fruit necessary for the life of men; and in order to do this, they made from her hair trees and flowers and grasses, from her skin the very fine grass and small flowers, from her eyes wells and fountains and small caverns, from her mouth rivers and great caverns, from her nose mountain valleys, and from her shoulders mountains. And this goddess sometimes wept at night, desiring to eat men's hearts, and would not be quiet until they were offered to her, nor would she bear fruit unless she was watered with the blood of men.

Above: Priests remove a human heart as an offering to the gods.

offerings on the great fire that the other gods built up on a stone altar. Tecuciztecatl burned fragrant incense and offered gold, gems, and quetzal feathers. Nanahuatzin could offer only reeds, pine needles, and cactus thorns dyed red with his blood. For incense, the humble god burned the scabs picked from his scarred body.

At midnight on the fourth day, the gods adorned the chosen ones for the sacrifice. They dressed Tecuciztecatl in rich garments and crowned him with a tall feathered headdress. As for poor, humble Nanahuatzin, they dressed him in a loincloth and headdress made of mere paper.

The gods formed two lines, one on each side of the altar. Tecuciztecatl and Nanahuatzin stood between the lines, facing the blazing bonfire. "Take courage, O Tecuciztecatl!" the watching gods shouted. "Cast yourself into the flames!"

The proud god took a step forward. He halted. The fire was a raging, terrifying inferno. Once more he advanced. Once more he stopped, struggling to overcome his terror. Finally, Tecuciztecatl turned tail and retreated. He could not jump into the fire.

Now the gods cried out to Nanahuatzin: "Quickly, you! Take heart! O Nanahuatzin, cast yourself into the flames!"

Nanahuatzin closed his eyes. His good heart gave him strength and power. Without hesitation, the little god ran and hurled himself into the center of the fire.

A great tongue of flame licked the heavens. There was a loud crackling and sizzling as the fire devoured Nanahuatzin's body. Beholding the humble god's heroic act, Tecuciztecatl was overcome with shame. With a loud cry, he too leaped into the bonfire.

The sacrifice was complete. Slowly the fire sputtered and died, leaving the world in darkness. The gods sat down and waited for the new sun to rise.

NANAHUATZIN . . . QUICKLY THREW AND CAST HIMSELF INTO THE FIRE.

~FLORENTINE CODEX

After a long time, a faint light reddened the sky like blood spreading out upon water. The gods looked to the east. Suddenly Nanahuatzin burst forth. The humble god had been transformed by his sacrifice. Now he was Tonatiuh, the life-giving sun. His shimmering rays warmed the earth, and his light was so dazzling that it was impossible to look into his face.

But what's this? On the heels of Tonatiuh came Tecuciztecatl, just as big and splendid! When the gods saw the two suns, they were outraged. How dare Tecuciztecatl shine as brightly as his courageous partner! Just then, a rabbit hopped by. One of the gods reached down and picked up the little animal. He threw the rabbit at the second sun, wounding Tecuciztecatl and dimming his light. Today you can still see the rabbit sprawled across the face of the full moon.

At last there was one new sun. But something was wrong. Tonatiuh simply hung on the eastern horizon, motionless. "How shall we live?" asked the gods. "How can time progress and the seasons pass if the sun does not move?" At last came the dreadful answer: They all must die in order to give the sun life.

One by one the gods removed their fine garments. They stood before Quetzalcoatl, and he cut out their hearts with his stone knife. The energy of their lifeblood nourished the sun. At last Tonatiuh began to follow his appointed path across the sky.

So it is that each day the sun emerges in the east to battle the darkness. And just as the gods sacrificed themselves to make Tonatiuh move, so the people give their blood to nourish him on his journey. At the end of his daily path, the sun is swallowed by the earth. Then the moon comes forth, lending us his feeble light while his partner travels back through the underworld to rise again the next morning.

The sun god Tonatiuh, with a symbol representing an earthquake on his back. According to one Aztec myth, an earthquake would destroy the world of the Fifth Sun.

Quetzalcoatl Visits the Underworld

AFTER THE GODS CREATED THE WORLD OF THE FIFTH Sun, they had to make people to live in it. The task of re-creating humanity went to Quetzalcoatl. That wise god journeyed to the underworld and brought back the bones of the people who had turned into fish at the end of the Fourth Sun. Then the gods used their own blood to bring the bones to life, creating a new race of humans.

This ancient tale gives us a window into the Aztecs' beliefs about the nature of the universe. According to their traditional tales, the universe consisted of three main regions: the upper world or heavens, the middle world or earthly level, and the underworld. Each of these regions was divided into several levels, which were inhabited by different gods and other supernatural beings. To create the new race of humans, Quetzalcoatl traveled down to the dark and gloomy ninth level of the underworld, known as Mictlan. There he had to outsmart the god of death, who was reluctant to release the bones of the human ancestors.

Opposite:
Quetzalcoatl's journey to the underworld restored life to the human race.

The story of the creation of humanity also helps explain the Aztecs' view of their role in the universe. Because people had been brought to life through the sacrifice of the gods, they had to give their own blood in return. Human sacrifice not only repaid an ancient debt. It was also essential to the continuation of life. The world of the Fifth Sun could not continue unless its creators were nourished with the magic essence of life found in human blood.

CAST *of* CHARACTERS

Quetzalcoatl (ket-sal-KO-waht) God of the morning star
Mictlantecuhtli (meek-tlan-tay-KWAH-tlee) God of the dead
Mictlancihuatl (meek-tlan-SEE-waht) Goddess of the dead
Cihuacoatl (see-wah-KO-waht) Patron goddess of midwives

FOUR AGES HAD COME AND GONE. A new world had been created after the Fourth Sun perished in the great flood. Still the gods were unhappy, because the world had no people to honor and serve them. So they called an assembly. "The earth has been spread out below the sky-waters," they said. "Who will settle there?"

Quetzalcoatl spoke up. "I will journey down to Mictlan," he said. "I will go to the Land of the Dead and bring back the bones of the fish-people. Their bones will become the ancestors of a new race of humans."

So Quetzalcoatl dove down through the body of the earth monster. He journeyed through the first eight layers of the underworld. Through fire and ice, past raging rivers, crashing mountains, and hungry monsters he traveled. At last he reached the ninth and bottom level of the underworld, Mictlan. This desolate realm is home to the spirits of those who died a natural death on earth. While the souls of dead warriors and other valiant people return to earth as birds and butter-flies, the spirits in Mictlan endure cold winds, dreadful famine, and endless darkness. Mictlan is also the place where the gods store the bones of past generations.

Quetzalcoatl bowed down before the thrones of Mictlantecuhtli and Mictlancihuatl, lord and lady of the dead land. "I have come for the precious bones that you are guarding," he told them.

"What will you do with them?" asked Mictlantecuhtli.

"The gods are sad because there are no people on the earth," answered Quetzalcoatl. "The bones will become the seeds of a new generation."

"Very well," said the crafty god of the dead. "You may take the bones. But first you must prove your worthiness by performing a sim-ple task. You must blow on my conch-shell trumpet as you carry it four times around my sacred realm."

Quetzalcoatl agreed to the dark lord's terms. But when he picked up the trumpet, he saw that it could not make a sound, because it had no holes. Quickly he summoned the worms and asked them to drill holes in the shell. He called for a swarm of bees, who flew inside it. Then the clever god paraded around the underworld, while the bees filled the horn with a loud buzzing sound.

Mictlantecuhtli was displeased, but he could not break his word. "Oh, very well! Take the bones!" he cried.

So Quetzalcoatl gathered up the bones of one man and one woman. He wrapped them in a bundle. Then he hurried off, before the lord of Mictlan could change his mind.

Meanwhile, Mictlantecuhtli sat muttering on his throne. Suddenly he shouted for his servants. "Quick! Quetzalcoatl is taking the pre-cious bones!" he cried. "You must dig a pit to trap him!"

The staring eyes of Mictlantecuhtli looked out over the cold and gloomy Land of the Dead.

The dark lord's servants hurried on ahead and dug a deep hole. As Quetzalcoatl ran from Mictlan, a flock of quail flew up and startled him. The god stumbled and fell into the pit, whacking his head. His precious bundle split open, and all the bones scattered. As Quetzalcoatl lay unconscious, the quail nibbled the broken bones to many different-sized pieces. (That is the reason people today come in so many different shapes and sizes.)

After a while Quetzalcoatl regained his senses. "What shall I do?" he cried. "Everything has gone wrong. The bones are ruined." Then a small voice inside the god's head whispered, "However it goes is how it goes. Make the best of it, and complete your journey."

So Quetzalcoatl gathered together all the scattered bits of bones. He carried them up through the nine levels of the underworld, through the earth, to the highest level of the heavens. There he gave them to Cihuacoatl, the ancient goddess who watches over childbirth.

Cihuacoatl put on her sacred eagle-feather headdress. She placed the bones in a bowl and ground them into a fine powder. One by one all the gods sprinkled drops of their blood over the vessel. Mixing together the powder and the blood, the goddess made a paste. She molded the sticky dough into a man and a woman.

The new race of humans sprang to life. "O gods, the people are born!" proclaimed Quetzalcoatl. "The people of the Fifth Sun have been given life through your sacrifices!"

Cihuacoatl sits on a throne above Tenochtitlán, keeping watch over the people she helped create.

THE AZTECS SPEAK
FRUITS *of the* EARTH

In "Quetzalcoatl Visits the Underworld," the god travels to the Land of the Dead in order to restore life to the world. To the Aztecs, that journey would have made perfect sense. According to their beliefs, life and death were simply two sides of the same reality. So were male and female, darkness and light, weakness and strength, creation and destruction. Everything in the world had two natures, which were both opposite and complementary (meaning that the two halves together made a whole).

A poem recited by modern-day descendants of the Aztecs in the Mexican state of Puebla may help us understand these age-old beliefs. The poet is reflecting on the complex connections between life and death. Humans must eat in order to live, but eating requires killing plants and animals, the "fruits of the earth." In this way life is born of death. The poem also reminds us that one day we will all return to the same earth that gave us life.

We live here on this earth
We are all fruits of the earth
the earth sustains us
we grow her, on the earth and lower
and when we die we wither in the earth
we are all fruits of the earth
We eat of the earth
because the earth eats us.

Above: An Aztec farmer tends a flourishing field of maize.

THE ORIGINS *of* CORN *and* PULQUE

Gifts from the Gods

ONCE THE GODS HAD RESTORED LIFE TO THE EARTH, they had to nourish their new creation. The most important divine gift to humans was maize, or corn. Maize was the central crop of early Mesoamerica. In Aztec times both nobles and commoners ate a diet based on maize prepared in various forms, such as soups, tortillas, and tamales. According to mythology, it was Quetzalcoatl who brought this vital food to the Aztec people.

Quetzalcoatl also gave humankind many other valuable gifts. Aztec myths credit him with introducing the calendar, establishing the priesthood, instructing people in the arts of weaving and stonework, and other acts to ensure humanity's survival. In addition, the beloved god helped give the Aztecs a gift that added pleasure to life: pulque.

Pulque (pronounced POOL-kay) is an alcoholic beverage made from the sap of the maguey plant. This sacred drink was believed to have magical properties that gave people strength and allowed them to

Opposite: This scene from a mural by Diego Rivera shows Aztecs working in the *chinampa* fields that lined the shores of Lake Texcoco.

experience other levels of reality. The Aztecs used pulque mainly in religious rituals. Nobles, warriors, nursing mothers, the elderly, and the sick were also permitted to sample it on occasion. Public drunkenness was strongly condemned and strictly punished, however. After the third offense, a person who was too fond of the potent powers of pulque could be put to death.

CAST *of* CHARACTERS

Quetzalcoatl (ket-sal-KO-waht) God of the morning star
Nanahuatl (nah-NAH-waht) God of lightning
Tlaloc (TLAH-lok) God of rain
Mayahuel (may-AH-well) Goddess of the maguey plant
Tzitzimitl (tzee-TZEE-meet) Queen of the star demons

Quetzalcoatl Discovers Corn

"WHAT SHALL THEY EAT?" The gods looked at one another and pondered the question. How would the new race of humans, the people of the Fifth Sun, find nourishment in a world washed clean of vegetation?

As so often happens, it was Quetzalcoatl who found the answer. Peering down from the heavens, the wise god saw a small red ant carrying a kernel of corn. Quetzalcoatl hurried down to the earth. "Where did you get that?" he asked the ant. "Tell me where you found that wonderful food."

At first, the ant refused to answer. It was afraid that the god would take away all its precious corn. But Quetzalcoatl was persistent, and when a mighty god demands an answer, a humble ant cannot long resist him. "Very well, I will show you the source of the corn," the ant said finally. "But you are much too big to enter the secret passageways where it lies hidden."

Instantly Quetzalcoatl changed himself into a little black ant. He followed the red ant over the hills and valleys of Anahuac, all the way to Food Mountain. The god saw hundreds of ants disappearing through a crack in the rock. Joining the line, he entered a long, narrow tunnel. He scurried down the passage to the center of the mountain. There he found a chamber filled with corn in four colors: white, black, red, and yellow. He also saw piles of beans, squash seeds, pepper seeds, and many other seeds and grains that the ants had hidden away when the world of the Fourth Sun was drowned in the great flood.

Quetzalcoatl discovered a precious supply of tasty, colorful corn.

Quetzalcoatl picked up a kernel of corn with his strong jaws. He labored back up the tunnel and lay down his burden. Down he went again, into the heart of the mountain. Back he came, with another kernel. Finally, the little black ant had gathered up a tidy mound of corn. Snap! He transformed himself back into a god. Then Quetzalcoatl carried the corn up to the heavens, where the other gods were waiting.

The gods tasted the corn. It was delicious! They chewed it up and placed the mash in the mouths of human infants. The hungry babies grew big and strong on the wholesome meal.

"Corn is the perfect food to strengthen and nourish the humans!" the gods declared. "But how will we get all of it out of Food Mountain?"

Again Quetzalcoatl thought that he had the answer. He wrapped a huge rope around Food Mountain and tried to pull it from the earth. The god strained and struggled, but even with his great powers, the gigantic rock would not budge.

So Nanahuatl, god of lightning, stepped forward. "I will crack it open," he declared, and he hurled his fiery weapon. There was a blinding flash as the lightning struck Food Mountain, splitting it wide open. All the gods cheered as the food came pouring out of the heart of the mountain.

But even as they celebrated, there arose a great commotion. Tlaloc, the god of rain who dwells on the mountaintops, was angered by the destruction of Food Mountain. Together with his four children, the rain gods of the four directions, he descended on the shattered pile of rocks. The swirling mass of gods snatched up all the corn kernels. They stole the beans and all the seeds and grains. Then they swept back to their hiding places high up in the mountains.

So it was that Quetzalcoatl found corn and other good things to nourish the people of the Fifth Sun. But the lords of rain still guard the food that was hidden in the mountain. Each year they give some of it back to humankind—some years more, other years less. That is why the people offer prayers and sacrifices to Tlaloc, asking him to send just the right amount of rain to make the crops grow in abundance.

The Joy of Pulque

Corn and beans fill the belly, but they cannot gladden the heart. Although the people of the Fifth Sun had everything they needed to survive, still they seemed unhappy. "We must find a way to give the humans joy," the gods said to one another. "Only then will they sing and dance and praise those who created them."

Quetzalcoatl floated on the wind, searching for an answer to the problem. What brings laughter and happiness? he wondered. Gradually his thoughts turned to the goddess Mayahuel. Long had he dreamed

The gods wanted to lift the spirits of humans, so they would sing and dance.

THE AZTECS SPEAK
A PRAYER for RAIN

The Aztecs worshipped a host of gods and goddesses associated with maize and other crops. Through rituals celebrated at various times throughout the growing season, they honored these deities and asked for their blessings. The following verses come from a long prayer to Tlaloc, god of rain. The prayer was recited as part of a special ceremony performed in times of drought.

Oh, the fruits of the earth lie panting;
the sister of the gods, the sustenances of life,
feebly drags herself along,
she is covered with dust, she is covered with cobwebs,
she is utterly worn and weary.

And behold, the people, the subjects, are perishing!
Their eyelids are puffy, their mouths dry as straw,
their bones are dessicated [dried up], and they are twisted and gaunt,
their lips are thin, their necks pale and scrawny. . . .

O Lord, Beloved Lord, O Provider!
May it be in your heart to grant, to give, to bring comfort to the earth
and all that lives from it, all that grows on it.
And you who inhabit the four quarters of the universe,
you the Lords of Verdure [greenness], you the Providers,
you the Lords of the Mountain Heights, you the Lords of the Cavernous Depths,
I call out, I cry out to you:
come, bring yourselves here,
comfort the people, slake the thirst of the earth;
the earth and the animals, the leaves and stalks
are watching and waiting and crying out.
O gods, Our Lords, make haste!

Above: This ancient wall painting shows Tlaloc carrying branches nourished by his gifts of rain.

Mayahuel wore a triangular cape and a headdress crowned with quetzal feathers.

of that maiden's sweet innocence and enchanting beauty. But Mayahuel dwelt in the sky, in a house fiercely guarded by her ancient grandmother Tzitzimitl. And Tzitzimitl was queen of the *tzitzimime*, the dreadful star demons who attack the sun each dawn, hoping to devour it completely.

Ha! Quetzalcoatl resolved to brave the wrath of Tzitzimitl! In a flash he soared to the sky-home of the *tzitzimime*. He found Mayahuel and her grandmother sleeping. Gently he awakened the lovely young maiden. "I have come to get you," he whispered. "Will you come with me down to the world of humans?"

The moment Mayahuel saw the god's handsome face, she consented. Quetzalcoatl lifted her upon his shoulders, and together they descended to the earth. When they touched the ground, the lovers entwined. They transformed themselves into a beautiful tree to hide from Tzitzimitl. The great tree had two branches, one belonging to Quetzalcoatl, the other to Mayahuel.

Soon Tzitzimitl awakened and saw that her granddaughter had left her. With her magic she knew at once what had happened. Screaming in rage, the ancient goddess summoned the *tzitzimime*. Then she swooped down to the earth with her dreadful servants to search for her disobedient granddaughter.

The demons soared over the fields, lakes, and mountains. When they came to the great tree, the two branches shuddered. Tzitzimitl peered at the tree suspiciously. Suddenly she recognized her granddaughter from a single white blossom on one of the branches. In a fit of fury, the old hag tore the branch from the

AS SOON AS THEY ARRIVED ON EARTH, THEY TRANSFORMED THEMSELVES INTO A TREE.

⌐ HISTOYRE DU MECHIQUE

tree. She shredded it to bits with her teeth and claws. She handed some of the pieces to her companions, who devoured them greedily. Then, as quickly as they had come, the demons flew back up to their home in the sky.

Now the branch of Quetzalcoatl stood alone on the broken tree. As soon as the *tzitzimime* were gone, the god changed back to his rightful form. Sadly he surveyed the broken bits of Mayahuel left behind by the ravenous demons. Then he tenderly gathered up the goddess's remains and buried them in the earth.

The sun shined. The rains fell. Tender green shoots pushed up from the ground where Mayahuel lay buried. In time the plant grew tall and strong. It grew into the first maguey!

The people of the earth soon discovered that the wonderful new plant was nearly as useful as corn. They used its fibers for weaving cloth and making rope, its thorns for needles, its leaves for paper and roofing. Its sweet white sap had healing powers. Best of all, when the sap of the maguey was left to ferment, it made a drink with magical powers. Those who drank the sacred pulque felt a surge of joy in their hearts. They wanted to sing and dance and laugh out loud. They wanted to celebrate the gods who created them. In pulque, the people at last knew happiness, just as Quetzalcoatl had intended.

After her death Mayahuel lived on in the marvelous maguey plant.

LIGHT *versus* DARKNESS

The Birth of Huitzilopochtli

THE AZTECS ADOPTED MOST OF THEIR GODS FROM the earlier peoples of Mesoamerica. One major exception was Huitzilopochtli. The Mexica people brought this fierce war god with them when they migrated down from the north and founded the Aztec Empire. As the Aztecs rose in power, their tribal god became one of their most important deities. Over time Huitzilopochtli took over some of the roles associated with earlier gods. In some myths, for example, he replaced Nanahuatzin as the god who emerged as the Fifth Sun.

According to mythology, Huitzilopochtli was an invincible warrior from the moment of his birth. While he was still in the womb, he learned that his jealous sister, the moon goddess Coyolxauhqui, planned to kill him and his mother. Bursting forth from his mother's body, he defeated his sister and her army of four hundred gods. (To the Aztecs, *four hundred* meant a number too great to be counted.) Then the infant god beheaded Coyolxauhqui and hurled her body down the side of a mountain.

Opposite: Coatlicue ("She of the Serpent Skirt") was a complex goddess associated with birth, motherhood, fertility, war, and human sacrifice.

Modern-day scholars believe that this gory story may represent the constant struggle between light and darkness. The newly born Huitzilopochtli conquered his sister and her army just as the rising sun triumphs over the moon and stars each morning. To ensure the sun's continued victory, the Aztecs waged an endless series of wars. Prisoners of war were often sacrificed in Huitzilopochtli's shrine atop the Great Temple pyramid in Tenochtitlán. The victims' blood and hearts were offered to the god, to nourish him for his daily battle against the forces of darkness. Then the lifeless bodies were rolled down the steps onto a huge circular image of Coyolxauhqui, repeating Huitzilopochtli's victory over his sister.

CAST *of* CHARACTERS

Coatlicue (ko-waht-LEE-kway) Goddess of agriculture; mother of Huitzilopochtli

Mixcoatl (meesh-KO-waht) God of hunting

Coyolxauhqui (koy-yol-SHAOW-kee) Goddess of fire and the moon

Cuahuitlicac (kwah-wee-TLEE-kak) One of the Four Hundred Southerners

Huitzilopochtli (weet-see-lo-POACH-tlee) God of war and the sun; patron god of the Aztecs

---

ON THE SLOPES OF COATEPEC, the Serpent Mountain, dwelt a woman named Coatlicue. This virtuous woman was the wife of Mixcoatl, god of hunting. She had borne her husband one daughter, Coyolxauhqui, and a multitude of gods known as the Four Hundred Southerners. After giving birth to all these children, Coatlicue had taken a vow of chastity. She would spend the remainder of her days as a priestess, doing holy work in the shrine at the top of the sacred mountain.

One day Coatlicue was sweeping out the shrine when a ball of brightly colored feathers came drifting down from the sky. The woman picked up the feathers and tucked them in the waistband of her skirt. After she had finished sweeping, she looked for them. They had vanished! Coatlicue did not know it, but the feathered ball had magical powers. From that moment, she was with child.

Soon Coyolxauhqui and the Four Hundred Southerners noticed their mother's belly beginning to swell. Their father, Mixcoatl, had been away for many months, so he could not have caused the pregnancy. There was only one possible explanation: Coatlicue must have broken her vow of chastity. Through her sinful act, she had insulted her husband and dishonored the entire family.

"Who has done this to you?" the gods asked their mother. "Who has made you pregnant?" When the poor woman could not answer, they became even more outraged.

A thorny plant sprouts from the head of an angry warrior.

"Brothers, our mother's sins have brought disgrace on our family," said Coyolxauhqui. "Why does she not reveal the name of her lover, so that we can punish him? There is only one way to deal with such wickedness. We must kill her!"

These bitter words fanned the anger of the gods into a raging fury. Together the Four Hundred Southerners vowed to join their sister in destroying their mother. First, they had to prepare for battle. They wound their hair around their heads in the style of warriors. They put on their thick armor and decorated it with streamers of colored paper. They tied war bells around the calves of their legs. Then they gathered up their bows and their sharp barbed arrows.

As the warriors were making their preparations, one slipped away from camp. Forgetting his vow to his sister and brothers, Cuahuitlicac made his way to Serpent Mountain. He found his mother in the shrine at the top and told her about the plot against her.

When Coatlicue learned of her children's cruel plan, she began to tremble with fear. Suddenly, she heard her unborn child speaking from her womb. "Do not be afraid," said the voice of Huitzilopochtli. "I know what I must do." Those confident words comforted the poor woman, so that at once her heart was peaceful and quiet.

The following morning, the Four Hundred Southerners moved out, with Coyolxauhqui guiding them. The mighty war party marched across the country, row after row, in an orderly formation. After a journey of several days, the warriors reached the foot of Serpent Mountain. Once again Cuahuitlicac sneaked off and ran ahead to warn his mother of their progress. "My brothers are climbing up the side of the mountain," he told her. "Now they have reached the top. They are drawing near. Here they are, with Coyolxauhqui leading them!"

At that very moment, Huitzilopochtli was born. The magnificent god sprang from his mother's womb fully armed and ready for battle. His arms and legs were painted blue. On his head was his blue-green headdress of hummingbird feathers. In his hands were his spears and his magical shield of eagle feathers. Most fearsome of all was his terrible spear-thrower, made from a living serpent. At a word

Huitzilopochtli carried a magical feathered shield and a deadly fire-serpent.

from the god, the fire-serpent burst into flames that burned as bright as lightning.

Huitzilopochtli lashed out with his lightning bolt. With one deadly stroke, he sliced Coyolxauhqui's head from her shoulders. He tossed the head into the sky, where it was born again as the moon. He hurled his sister's body down the mountainside. As it fell, it broke into pieces, so that her arms and legs landed in different places.

Then the god turned his divine anger against his half brothers, the Four Hundred Southerners. He drove them off the mountaintop, and as they fled, he pursued them like a hunter chasing rabbits. In vain the warriors tried to rally against him. In vain they clashed their shields and rattled their bells, hoping to frighten him. They could do nothing to turn aside the fierce and fearless warrior.

Four times Huitzilopochtli made his brothers run around the base of the mountain, until they stumbled and begged for mercy. A very few managed to escape back to the south. The wrathful god caught all the others. He struck them with his fire-serpent and completely obliterated them.

That is how Huitzilopochtli defeated his sister Coyolxauhqui and the Four Hundred Southerners. Every day we witness a renewal of this divine combat. For each dawn the sun springs newborn from the body of the earth. Each morning he triumphs over the moon and scatters the unnumbered stars to the far corners of the sky.

THE ORIGINS *of the* AZTEC PEOPLE

The Great Migration

LIKE THEIR GODS, THE AZTECS' MYTHS WERE LARGELY adopted from the earlier peoples of Mesoamerica. There were a few essentially original Aztec myths, however. Most of these related to the beginnings of the Mexica people and their migration to Tenochtitlán, the swampy island that would become the heart of their empire.

The Aztecs told many different versions of their migration myth. According to the best-known account, the Mexica once lived in a mysterious place far to the north known as Aztlan, or "Place of Herons." One day Huitzilopochtli commanded them to journey south to a distant land where he would make them the rulers of a mighty nation. With the god leading the way, the people set out on their long, difficult migration. After many years they reached the shores of Lake Texcoco in the Valley of Mexico. There they saw a huge eagle perched on a cactus, a sign that they had reached the "promised land."

The Aztec migration story interweaves history and mythology.

Opposite: La Fiesta del Maiz ("Corn Festival") by Diego Rivera celebrates the agricultural riches of the Valley of Mexico.

Some of the places described in the story are imaginary, while others were real towns and cities in early Mesoamerica. Some of the episodes echo the ancient stories of other peoples, while others are probably based on historical events. To the Aztecs, this creative retelling of history was sacred and true. Children studied the migration story in school, poets recited it in verses, and artists recorded it in codices. Passed down through all these different avenues, the tale of their ancestors' rise to glory was a source of pride from generation to generation. Most importantly, the Aztecs regarded the heroic story as proof that it was their divine destiny to rule over all the conquered peoples of Mesoamerica.

CAST *of* CHARACTERS

Huitzilopochtli (weet-see-lo-POACH-tlee) God of war and the sun; patron god of the Aztecs
Malinalxochitl (mah-lee-nahl-SHOW-cheet) Evil sorceress; sister of Huitzilopochtli
Copil (KO-peel) Evil sorcerer; son of Malinalxochitl
Achitometl (ah-chee-TOE-mate) King of the ancient city of Culhuacan

The Journey Begins

IN THE DISTANT PAST, in the days of the grandfathers of the grandfathers, the Mexica people lived far to the north in Aztlan. This ancient city on a lake was a wonderful place. The waters abounded with fish and birds, and the fields produced rich harvests of corn. The people were never sad or hungry, and they never grew old.

When they became weary, they simply climbed a tall mountain in the center of Aztlan. The higher they climbed, the younger they became. When they reached the age they desired, they rested awhile and then came down from the mountain.

The Mexica shared their blessed homeland with six other tribes. One by one the people of those tribes grew restless and left Aztlan. Finally, there was no one left but the Mexica. For more than three hundred years, they dwelt in the northern paradise alone.

Huitzilopochtli told the Mexica that they would establish a great empire in the place where an eagle perched on a cactus.

One night Huitzilopochtli appeared to one of his priests in a dream. "In the south there is an island in the middle of blue waters," the great god whispered. "On the island grows a tall cactus. On the cactus stands an eagle, basking in the rays of the sun. In his talons the eagle holds a small, precious bird. There, in your new home, your destiny awaits you. There you will become the mightiest of all nations."

The Mexica were overjoyed when they learned of the god's message. Quickly they prepared to leave their homeland. Four priests would serve as leaders during the journey. The priests would carry the sacred image of Huitzilopochtli on their backs. The god would speak to them, and they would relay his pronouncements to the rest of the travelers. In this way Huitzilopochtli would guide his chosen people across the wilderness to the place of destiny.

Wonders and Hardships

The Mexica left Aztlan in search of a new home. This illustration from an Aztec codex shows Huitzilopochtli (the small head at the right) giving directions to his people.

For many generations the Mexica wandered through strange lands. They endured hunger and thirst, plagues and tempests, locusts and hailstorms. Scorned by the inhabitants of the lands through which they passed, they fought many small skirmishes and larger battles.

From time to time, the wanderers stopped to rest in fertile places. At each stop they erected a temple to Huitzilopochtli. They built homes and planted maize and other crops to sustain them. After a while—sometimes ten years, sometimes as long as twenty—their god would command them to move on, and they would obey him. Often they left behind the old, sick, and weary when they resumed their journey. In this way the Mexica founded many towns and populated many places during their long migration.

After a number of years, the travelers came to a place called Patzcuaro, where they found a clear lake filled with all kinds of fish. The priests asked Huitzilopochtli if they could leave part of their group in this pleasant land. The god granted their request and told them how to accomplish it. The next day, as some of the men and women were bathing in the lake, others sneaked up and stole their cloaks, skirts, and blouses. When the bathers came out of the water, they could not find their clothes. They hurried back to camp and saw that it was abandoned. Naked and forsaken, they decided to remain in

Patzcuaro. That is why the people of that land used to walk about with their private parts uncovered.

The Mexica traveled on to the town now known as Malinalco. There they abandoned the sorceress Malinalxochitl, who was a sister of Huitzilopochtli. Malinalxochitl was very beautiful but also very cruel. She was so skilled in magic that she could command deadly snakes, scorpions, and spiders to kill anyone who angered her. The priests had begged Huitzilopochtli to rid them of this evil woman. The god had told them to abandon Malinalxochitl while she lay sleeping. When the woman awakened and saw that she had been tricked, she wept in anger. Cursing her brother's name, she settled in the town that bears her name. To this day her descendants in Malinalco have the reputation of being sorcerers.

Next the Mexica stopped in Coatepec, the land of Huitzilopochtli's birth. There they built a dam across a river. The waters overflowed, flooding the plains. Soon reeds, rushes, willows, and cypresses crowded the banks of the lake they had created. Fish multiplied in the waters, attracting many different kinds of waterbirds. "O great Huitzilopochtli, this is surely the land that you promised," the people sang happily. "This will be the capital of your kingdom."

Huitzilopochtli became enraged when he heard their foolish singing. "Are you greater than I? Do you dare give opinions on those things that I have determined?" he thundered. In his fury the god punched a hole in the dam, and the waters poured out. All the plants and trees withered. All the fish perished, and the birds flew away.

Frightened and humbled, the Mexica continued on their journey. After many more years of wandering, they came to

Priests communicated with the image of Huitzilopochtli and passed on his messages to the wandering people.

Chapultepec, on the shores of Lake Texcoco. Then Huitzilopochtli spoke to the people, warning them to take courage. The promised land was near, but before they reached it, they would face fierce opposition from a new enemy. Malinalxochitl, the evil woman abandoned earlier in their travels, had borne a son named Copil. The sorceress had raised this terrible youth to despise his uncle. She had taught him all her tricks and witchcraft. Now Copil was coming with a gigantic army to take vengeance on Huitzilopochtli and his followers.

Quickly the Mexica prepared their spears and arrows. When Copil's army attacked, they fought back courageously. They were greatly outnumbered, but somehow they managed to hack their way through the enemy ranks to safety.

Meanwhile, Huitzilopochtli chased after Copil and killed him. The god slashed open his nephew's chest and tore out his heart. He gave this to his chief priest, instructing the man to cast it out over Lake Texcoco. The heart of the slain sorcerer fell on a rock on an island in the middle of the lake. The place where it landed would become the heart of the Aztec Empire.

The Fulfillment of the Prophecy

Copil had been defeated, but the Mexica people were weary and discouraged. Surrounded by enemies, they turned once again to Huitzilopochtli. "Be of strong heart!" their god told them. "Send envoys to Achitometl, king of Culhuacan. Ask him to give you a place in his country to settle."

So the people sent messengers to the great city of Culhuacan. Huitzilopochtli softened the king's heart, and Achitometl ordered his chieftains to give the Mexica whatever they requested. But the chiefs

THE AZTECS SPEAK
"WHO ARE YOU?"

According to the Aztecs' sacred history, their ancestors endured many hardships during their long journey to the promised land. Often their troubles came at the hands of earlier migrants who had reached Mexico before them. This ancient song tells the story of the Aztecs' rejection by the people they would one day conquer.

As they came,
as they went along their road,
they were no longer received anywhere,
they were rejected everywhere,
no one knew their face.
Everywhere they were asked:
"Who are you?
From where do you come?"
Thus nowhere could they settle,
they were always thrown out,
everywhere were they persecuted.
They passed through Coatepec,
they passed through Tollan [Tula]. . . .
Next, to Chapultepec
where many peoples came to settle. . . .
Mexico did not yet exist,
there still were fields of bulrushes and reeds
where now is Mexico.

Above: The leading priest in this illustration from an Aztec codex is carrying the sacred image of Huitzilopochtli on his back.

The king's advisers hoped that their unwelcome guests would be wiped out by poisonous snakes and lizards.

wanted only to be rid of the ragged band of wanderers. They debated how to manage that while still obeying the king's orders. Finally, they told the Mexica that they could settle in Tizapan, a barren wasteland infested with poisonous snakes and lizards.

The Mexica had no choice but to accept the offer. When they reached Tizapan and saw all the deadly reptiles, they were horrified. Again Huitzilopochtli spoke to the priests. He told them how to catch the snakes and lizards and eat them. Soon the people became so fond of boiled and roasted reptiles that they consumed nearly all of them. In fact, they were so contented in their new home that they never wished to leave it. That did not please Huitzilopochtli. He had led his people through the wilderness to found a mighty nation. He intended to make them lords over all the nations, not over snakes and lizards. So the great god devised a plan to put an end to the peace and quiet.

A time came when Achitometl sent his chiefs to see how the people of Tizapan were faring. The king's men expected to find the wretched settlers nearly wiped out by the poisonous reptiles. Instead, they saw a splendid temple, neatly cultivated fields, and snakes boiling in cook pots. When they returned with their report, the king was amazed and a little frightened by the remarkable strangers. He quickly granted the Mexica's one request: that he send his beloved daughter to become the bride of their god Huitzilopochtli.

When the princess arrived in Tizapan, the Mexica did as their god had commanded them. They placed her on an altar and sacrificed her. After the girl was dead, they removed her skin. They draped it over a young priest as a sacred costume. Then they invited the king of Culhuacan to come to a festival honoring their new goddess.

The priest was dressed in the skin of the king's slain daughter.

King Achitometl accepted the invitation. Bearing offerings of fine food, flowers, and incense, he and his nobles traveled to Tizapan. There they were greeted as honored guests. They rested and they dined. Then the Mexica invited the king to worship in the temple.

Achitometl entered the inner sanctuary. Stumbling about in the darkness, he presented his offerings. When he tossed the incense into the fire, the flames shot upward, illuminating the chamber. The king beheld the sacred image of Huitzilopochtli. Then he saw the priest seated beside the idol, adorned in the skin of his daughter.

With a scream of horror, Achitometl ran from the temple. "Come, my followers!" he shouted. "They have killed and skinned my daughter! Death and destruction to these fiends and their vile customs. Let us slay them. Let us leave not a trace of them."

Quickly the people of Culhuacan raised the alarm throughout their city. Hordes of armed warriors came running. The Mexica hastily grabbed their weapons and retreated toward the lake. Some of the men held off the attackers, while others lashed together their spears and shields. With the help of these crude rafts, the people crossed to the island in the middle of the water. Cold and wet, they spent the rest of the day huddled among the reeds and rushes.

That night Huitzilopochtli heard the weeping of the women and children. Moved by their despair, he spoke to his priests. "Console the people," he said. "Tell them that they must endure their afflictions a little while longer. Soon they will find their heart's desire."

The next day the Mexica dried their clothes and cleaned their weapons. Then they trudged on through the marshes, seeking the consolation their god had promised them. At last they came upon a beautiful spring running with cool, clear water. Beside the spring stood an immense prickly pear cactus, sprouting from the heart of Copil. A giant eagle was perched among the thorns, with his wings stretched out toward the sun. In his talons the eagle held a small bird with shining feathers.

> OUT OF [COPIL'S] HEART SPROUTED THE PRICKLY PEAR CACTUS.
> ⌐*HISTORIA DE LAS INDIAS DE NUEVA ESPAÑA*

The Mexica wept with joy at the fulfillment of the ancient prophecy. At long last they had reached the end of their journey. And when the eagle saw the people, he bowed his head in their direction.

So it was that Huitzilopochtli led his weary people to their destined

Huitzilopochtli's promise was fulfilled when the Mexica built their new capital on an island in the midst of blue waters.

homeland. There they would build a great city and name it Tenochtitlán, "Place of the Prickly Pear Cactus." With the might of their arms and the courage of their hearts, they would conquer all nations near and distant. Tenochtitlán would become the queen of all cities and the heart of the mighty Aztec Empire. And through their deeds, Huitzilopochtli, lord of the Aztecs, would achieve everlasting fame and glory.

THE END *of the* WORLD

Tales of the Conquest

THE MOST TRAGIC EVENT IN AZTEC HISTORY WAS THE Spanish Conquest. In April 1519 Hernán Cortés and an army of about six hundred conquistadors ("conquerors") landed on the east coast of Mexico. Cortés had heard rumors of a splendid inland empire. Eager to get his hands on its treasures, he marched his forces toward Tenochtitlán. In a little more than two years, the Spaniards gained complete control of the magnificent Aztec capital and all its territories.

How could such a small army topple such a mighty empire? Early Spanish accounts gave the credit to Cortés's brilliant leadership and superior weapons. Modern-day historians point to a number of other significant factors. First, more than 100,000 warriors from tribes throughout Mesoamerica fought for the Spaniards, hoping to free themselves from Aztec domination. In addition, an epidemic of small-pox—a deadly disease brought by the Europeans—weakened or killed millions of people in and around Tenochtitlán. It is also possible that

Opposite:
The people of the Fifth Sun fight the Spanish invaders, in this dramatic panel from a Diego Rivera mural.

the Aztecs' religious beliefs contributed to their downfall. According to some accounts, the emperor Moctezuma may have believed that the strange light-skinned foreigners were long-lost gods, returning as foretold in ancient prophecies. The Spaniards' behavior soon proved him wrong. By that time, however, the Aztecs had become too weak to overcome the invaders and their native allies.

Our retelling of the events surrounding the fall of the Aztec Empire is based on accounts written by the Aztecs themselves. Shortly after the surrender of Tenochtitlán, native survivors began to record their memories of the Spanish invasion in poems, chronicles, and plays. These sources offer a dramatic look at the history of the Conquest from the viewpoint of the conquered. They also show us how the Aztecs drew on their ancient beliefs to explain the sudden catastrophic end of their world. In accounts blending history and mythology, the Aztec writers blame the Conquest not only on Spanish armies but on spiritual forces set in motion at the very beginning of the world.

CAST *of* CHARACTERS

Huitzilopochtli (weet-see-lo-POACH-tlee) God of war and the sun; patron god of the Aztecs

Xiuhtecuhtli (she-wah-tay-KWAH-tlee) Ancient fire god

Moctezuma (mock-tuh-ZOO-muh) Aztec emperor; also known as Montezuma II

Quetzalcoatl (ket-sal-KO-waht) God of the morning star

Tezcatlipoca (tez-kaht-lee-PO-kah) God of the night and darkness

Hernán Cortés (kor-TEZ) Spanish explorer and conqueror

The Eight Omens

TEN YEARS BEFORE THE ARRIVAL OF THE SPANIARDS, the people of Tenochtitlán began to see troubling signs of the terrors to come.

The first omen was a great flame that blazed in the night sky. It was shaped like a pyramid, with its base against the ground and its peak reaching up to touch the heavens. It seemed to bleed fire, drop by drop, as if the sky itself were wounded.

The second omen was this: The temple of Huitzilopochtli burst into flames, though no one had set it afire. When the people threw water on the blaze, the tongues of flame leaped even higher. Thus the home of the great warrior who vanquished the powers of darkness each morning was burned to ashes.

The third omen was this: A lightning bolt struck the temple of Xiuhtecuhtli, oldest of all the gods. Only a light rain was falling, and there was no sound of thunder. The people said that the temple had been struck by a blow from the sun.

The fourth omen was this: A comet flashed across the sky in broad daylight. It raced from the place where the sun sets to the place where the sun rises, defying the natural order. The comet's three long tails showered sparks like red-hot coals, lighting the sky with their splendor.

The fifth omen was this: The wind lashed Lake Texcoco, the great body of water that surrounded and sustained the capital. The lake boiled with rage, foaming up to a great height. Then the waters dashed against the city, washing away half the houses.

The sixth omen was this: The people heard the voice of a woman weeping in the darkness. Night after night she haunted the city, crying out mournfully, "O my beloved sons, we are lost! Where can I hide you?"

Moctezuma feared that the comet blazing across the night sky was a sign of his empire's downfall.

The seventh omen was this: The men who fish in the lake snared a strange ash-colored bird, resembling a crane. On the crown of its head was a clear black mirror. The fishermen brought the wondrous bird to the emperor's palace. Moctezuma looked into the mirror and saw the night sky and all its stars. He looked a second time and saw a host of men, armed like warriors. They were approaching swiftly in well-ordered ranks, some walking, others riding on the backs of huge hornless deer. The vision filled the emperor with dread. He called for his magicians to explain it, but when they looked in the mirror, the image had disappeared.

The eighth and final omen was this: Deformed men with two heads but only one body appeared in the streets of the city. The people brought the strange creatures to the palace. The moment Moctezuma beheld them, they vanished.

All these wonders filled the Aztecs' hearts with terror. The people wept and shouted, and the priests offered the hearts of many captives. Meanwhile, Moctezuma sat on his throne, brooding. The emperor knew that the world of the Fifth Sun was destined to perish, just like the four worlds before it. If the omens were signs that the end was coming, there was nothing he or anyone else could do to prevent it.

The Fall of Tenochtitlán

The sacred books tell us that long ago, Quetzalcoatl was forced into exile through the treachery of his brother Tezcatlipoca. The beloved god sailed away to the east on a raft made of serpents. But Quetzalcoatl made a promise before he left Mexico. He would return one day to vanquish Tezcatlipoca and reclaim his ancient kingdom.

So it was with great foreboding that the emperor Moctezuma heard the words of a messenger from a village to the east. "I saw towers or small mountains floating on the waves of the sea," the man reported. "The mountains bore a race of humans like none I have ever seen before. The men had long beards and yellow hair and skin as white as the flowers of the maguey."

This news distressed the emperor even more than the ten years of omens that had preceded it. It was the very year predicted for the return of Quetzalcoatl. Had the god crossed the sea with his divine attendants to overthrow the old order and reclaim his throne?

Moctezuma decided to dispatch messengers with gifts for the strangers, just in case they were gods. He ordered his craftsmen to fashion copies of the ancient raiment worn by Quetzalcoatl: a serpent mask made of turquoise, a necklace with a gold disk in the center, a jade bracelet with little gold bells, a shield decorated with gold and

The emperor sent lavish gifts, including a turquoise mask of Quetzalcoatl, to the strange yellow-haired visitors.

The emperor's gifts only made the Spaniards bolder and more greedy.

mother-of-pearl and quetzal feathers. These treasures were packed in baskets, along with many other precious objects. Then the envoys journeyed to the coast, where they presented the emperor's gifts to Hernán Cortés, captain of the Spaniards.

When the messengers returned, they made their report to Moctezuma. They told him about the Spaniards' iron clothes and weapons. They described the thundering cannon that could shatter a tree into splinters and the tall creatures resembling deer, which carried the men wherever they wanted. Amazed and frightened, the emperor ordered his most gifted sorcerers to use their magic to send the mysterious strangers back to their own land. The magicians' spells failed completely. From then on, Moctezuma sat on his throne, paralyzed with fear and uncertainty. He did nothing but wait as Cortés and his army marched inland, slaughtering many people and making allies of others.

At length the Spaniards reached the capital. The emperor himself went out to meet them. He did not resist when the men he had mistaken for gods took him prisoner in his own palace. He did not protest even when they seized his gold like hungry pigs gobbling up their supper. For many months the greedy strangers ruled over the capital, using the captive emperor as their puppet. Finally, the Aztec warriors took up their spears and shields and cast out their captors.

[MOCTEZUMA] WENT OUT TO MEET THEM. . . . HE SHOWERED GIFTS UPON THEM.

~FLORENTINE CODEX

Moctezuma died in the fighting. Some say that he was put to death by the Spaniards, others that he was slain by his own people as a coward and traitor to his country.

For a brief time after the overthrow of the Spaniards, there was rejoicing in Tenochtitlán. Then a terrible plague struck the city. The victims were wracked with coughs and covered from head to foot with agonizing sores. Many died before the disease released its grip on the people.

While the city's defenses were weakened, the Spaniards returned with a new and even larger army. They surrounded Tenochtitlán with their warships and cannons. They destroyed the aqueduct that carried freshwater from the mainland. For eighty days, they held the capital under siege. The people were tormented with thirst and hunger. They

The Spanish conquerors disposed of the bodies of Moctezuma and his noble followers.

ate lizards, corncobs, and salt grasses. Some chewed on deer hide. Some even ate dirt. No matter how weak they grew, the Aztec warriors still fought with courage each time the enemy raided the suffering city.

One night a great flame appeared in the heavens, wheeling around like a whirlwind. It circled the city, then moved out over the middle of the lake, where it suddenly vanished. The weary people watched the omen in silence. The next day they surrendered. Cortés drove them out of Tenochtitlán, slaughtering some and making slaves of others. He stripped the city of all its treasures. Then he demolished the proud capital and built a Spanish city known as Mexico City on the ruins.

The omens had been fulfilled. The temples and palaces lay in ruins, and the people were scattered. Even the gods seemed to have forsaken them, as the Spaniards condemned the sacred texts to the fire. But Aztec priests and other learned people who had survived the fall of Tenochtitlán would compose new books, recalling the spirit of the people and the glory of the empire. Their children and grandchildren and great-grandchildren would keep alive the ancient traditions. There are even some who still believe that Quetzalcoatl will truly return one day, bringing a new age of peace and prosperity.

THE AZTECS SPEAK
SONGS *of* SORROW

After the Spanish Conquest, Aztec writers lamented the destruction of Tenochtitlán. An unknown poet wrote the following song sometime around the late sixteenth century. The first verse refers to Tlatelolco, the once-great market district in Tenochtitlán where the Aztecs made a last stand against the Spaniards in August 1521. It is believed that as many as 40,000 Aztec men, women, and children were killed at Tlatelolco.

Nothing but flowers and songs of sorrow
are left in Mexico and Tlatelolco,
where once we saw warriors and wise men.

We know it is true
that we must perish,
for we are mortal men.
You, the Giver of Life,
you have ordained it.

We wander here and there
in our desolate poverty.
We are mortal men.
We have seen bloodshed and pain
where once we saw beauty and valor.

We are crushed to the ground;
we lie in ruins.
There is nothing but grief and suffering
in Mexico and Tlatelolco,
where once we saw beauty and valor.

Above: A sixteenth-century codex shows the victorious Spaniards
forcing Aztec nobles to turn over their riches.

GLOSSARY

Anahuac (ah-NAH-wahk) the Aztec name for the Valley of Mexico; *Anahuac* (or *Cemanahuac*) means "Land between the Waters"

city-states independent states, each made up of a city and its surrounding territory

codices (KO-dih-seez) early Aztec religious or historical texts consisting of pictographs (word pictures) painted on paper made from bark or deerskin, which were folded accordion style; the singular form is *codex*

deities gods, goddesses, and other divine beings

legend a traditional story that may involve ordinary mortals as well as divine beings and may be partly based on real people and events

maize a tall variety of corn native to the Americas

Mesoamerica a part of Central America that was occupied by the Aztecs and other peoples in the days before European contact; Mesoamerica included most of modern-day Mexico, Guatemala, and Belize, as well as parts of Honduras, El Salvador, Nicaragua, and Costa Rica

Mexica (meh-SHE-kah) the people who migrated from the north and settled in the Valley of Mexico, founding the Aztec Empire

Mictlan (MEEK-tlan) the lowest level of the Aztec underworld

mythology the whole body of myths belonging to a people

myths traditional stories about gods and other divine beings, which were developed by ancient cultures to explain the mysteries of the physical and spiritual worlds

Nahuatl (NAH-waht) the ancient language of the Mexica

Mictlantecuhtli, king of Mictlan, the lowest level of the underworld

people, which became the dominant language of Mesoamerica; Nahuatl is still spoken in Mexico and many parts of Central America

patron a god or goddess that was believed to be the special protector of a group of people

prophecy a foretelling of something that will happen in the future

pulque (POOL-kay) an alcoholic beverage made from the fermented sap of the maguey plant, which was drunk or sacrificed as part of religious rituals

quetzal (ket-SAHL) a Central American bird with bright green feathers

siege a battle tactic in which an attacker surrounds a fortress or city, cutting off supplies to force the enemy to surrender

tzitzimime (tzee-tzee-ME-me) evil star demons who battle the sun at dawn and dusk and devour it completely during solar eclipses

AZTEC WRITING *and* TEXTS

The Spanish conquerors of Mexico destroyed nearly all of the Aztec codices (texts consisting mainly of word pictures known as pictographs). Today most of our written information about Aztec beliefs and mythology comes from books written shortly after the Conquest. These include traditional stories collected by Spanish chroniclers as well as new codices written by native people educated in Spanish colonial schools. Some of these post-Conquest texts were written in Spanish, others in Nahuatl, the ancient language of the Mexica people.

Above: A page from an early Mesoamerican codex

The myths retold in this book are based mainly on the following sources:

Crónica Mexicana ("Mexican Chronicles")
Crónica Mexicana was written around 1598 by Hernando Alvarado Tezozomoc, a grandson of the Aztec emperor Moctezuma. The text covers Aztec history from the late fourteenth century through the Spanish Conquest.

Crónica Mexicayotl ("Chronicles in the Mexican Manner")
Mythology and history overlap in these accounts of the origins of the Aztec people, the founding of Tenochtitlán, and other events through the Spanish Conquest. The text was written in Nahuatl around 1609 by Hernando Alvarado Tezozomoc, the author of *Crónica Mexicana*.

Historia General de las Cosas de Nueva España ("General History of the Things of New Spain"); also known as the *Florentine Codex*
Fray Bernardino de Sahagún was a Spanish missionary who came to Mexico in 1529. He spent much of the next twenty-five years interviewing Aztec elders about their traditional beliefs and myths. Native scribes recorded the interviews, and Sahagún edited those records to produce this encyclopedia of Aztec thought.

Historia de las Indias de Nueva España ("History of the Indies of New Spain")
Diego Durán emigrated with his parents from Spain to Mexico around 1540. He later became a Dominican friar (a member of a Catholic religious order) and devoted his life to converting the

Mexican people from their ancient faith to Christianity. His lengthy book on Aztec history and culture includes his Spanish translations of a now-lost Aztec history written in Nahuatl.

Historia de los Mexicanos por sus Pinturas ("History of the Mexica Peoples as Told by Their Paintings")
This text on Aztec mythology was written by the Spanish priest and scholar Andrés de Olmos in the 1530s. It may have been based on a painted codex that has since been lost.

Histoyre du Mechique ("History of the Mexicans")
A French scholar named André Thévet produced this translation of a now-lost sixteenth-century Spanish manuscript on Aztec mythology. The narrative includes the story of the goddess Tlaltecuhtli, whose body became the earth during the age of the Fifth Sun.

Leyenda de los Soles ("Legend of the Suns")
This is the only surviving version of the Aztec creation story written in Nahuatl. It was produced by an unknown Spanish-educated Aztec author in 1558.

To FIND OUT MORE

BOOKS

Andréadis, Ianna, and Elisa Amado. *Sun Stone Days/Tonaltin/Días de Piedra*. Toronto: Groundwood Books, 2005.

Boone, Elizabeth Hill. *The Aztec World*. Washington, DC: Smithsonian Books, 1994.

Dalal, Anita. *Myths of Pre-Columbian America*. Austin, TX: Raintree Steck-Vaughn, 2001.

Greger, C. Shana. *The Fifth and Final Sun: An Ancient Aztec Myth of the Sun's Origin*. New York: Houghton Mifflin, 1994.

Jones, David M. *Mythology of the Aztecs and Maya*. London: Southwater, 2003.

León-Portilla, Miguel, ed. *The Broken Spears: The Aztec Account of the Conquest of Mexico*. Boston: Beacon Press, 1992.

Lourie, Peter. *Hidden World of the Aztec*. Honesdale, PA: Boyds Mills, 2006.

Schuman, Michael A. *Mayan and Aztec Mythology*. Berkeley Heights, NJ: Enslow, 2001.

Stein, R. Conrad. *The Aztec Empire*. Cultures of the Past series. New York: Benchmark Books, 1996.

West, David. *Graphic Mythology: Mesoamerican Myths*. New York: Rosen, 2006.

WEB SITES

Aztec Mythology at
http://www.cis.yale.edu/ynhti/curriculum/units/1994/3/94.03.03.x.html
This site was created for teachers, but young readers will find the information on Aztec religious beliefs and practices clear and informative. Site creator Lorna Dilts, from the Yale–New Haven Teachers Institute, has included retellings of three Aztec creation myths.

The Aztecs at
http://home.freeuk.net/elloughton13/aztecs.htm
This bright and colorful site was created by Derek Allen, former headmaster of Snaith Primary School in England. The site explores

the Aztec world through stories, pictures, and interactive games. The text is available in both English and Spanish.

Aztecs at Mexicolore at
http://www.mexicolore.co.uk/index.php?one=azt
This London-based educational Web site is dedicated to promoting Mexico's Aztec heritage. Click on the links for information about Aztec life and religion plus retellings of several myths and legends.

Encyclopedia Mythica: Aztec Mythology at
http://www.pantheon.org/areas/mythology/americas/aztec
This online encyclopedia offers more than ninety brief articles on the Aztec gods and goddesses.

The Gods of Aztec Mythology at
http://www.godchecker.com/pantheon/aztec-mythology.php
Godchecker is an online encyclopedia with a great sense of humor! The site includes a brief introduction to Aztec mythology plus lively articles on "a host of interesting Gods with completely unpronounceable names."

Museo del Templo Mayor at
http://archaeology.asu.edu/tm/index2.htm
The Templo Mayor Museum in Mexico City has eight halls exhibiting thousands of objects uncovered at the site of the main temple in the Aztec capital at Tenochtitlán (present-day Mexico City). Click on the links for photographs of ancient sculptures, paintings, drawings, and sacrificial offerings to the gods.

SELECTED BIBLIOGRAPHY

Bierhorst, John, trans. *History and Mythology of the Aztecs: The Codex Chimalpopoca.* Tucson: University of Arizona Press, 1992.

Bierhorst, John, ed. *The Hungry Woman: Myths and Legends of the Aztecs.* New York: William Morrow, 1984.

Carrasco, Davíd. *Daily Life of the Aztecs: People of the Sun and Earth.* Westport, CT: Greenwood Press, 1998.

Carrasco, Davíd, and Eduardo Matos Moctezuma. *Moctezuma's Mexico: Visions of the Aztec World.* Niwot, CO: University Press of Colorado, 1992.

Caso, Alfonso. *The Aztecs: People of the Sun.* Translated by Lowell Dunham. Norman, OK: University of Oklahoma Press, 1958.

Durán, Diego. *The Aztecs: The History of the Indies of New Spain.* Translated by Doris Heyden and Fernando Horcasitas. New York: Orion Press, 1964.

Ferguson, Diana. *Tales of the Plumed Serpent: Aztec, Inca and Mayan Myths.* London: Collins and Brown, 2000.

León-Portilla, Miguel, ed. *The Broken Spears: The Aztec Account of the Conquest of Mexico.* Boston: Beacon Press, 1992.

León-Portilla, Miguel. *Pre-Columbian Literatures of Mexico.* Norman, OK: University of Oklahoma Press, 1969.

Markman, Roberta H., and Peter T. Markman. *The Flayed God: The Mesoamerican Mythological Tradition.* San Francisco, CA: Harper San Francisco, 1992.

Phillips, Charles. *The Mythology of the Aztec and Maya.* London: Southwater, 2006.

Read, Kay Almere, and Jason J. González. *Handbook of Mesoamerican Mythology.* Santa Barbara, CA: ABC-CLIO, 2000.

Soustelle, Jacques. *Daily Life of the Aztecs.* Translated by Patrick O'Brian. London: Phoenix Press, 1995.

Taube, Karl. *Aztec and Maya Myths.* Austin: University of Texas Press, 1993.

NOTES *on* QUOTATIONS

Quoted passages in sidebars come from the following sources:

"The Earth Monster," page 40, from the *Histoyre du Mechique*, in Roberta H. Markman and Peter T. Markman, *The Flayed God: The Mesoamerican Mythological Tradition* (San Francisco, CA: Harper San Francisco, 1992).

"Fruits of the Earth," page 49, in Davíd Carrasco, *Daily Life of the Aztecs: People of the Sun and Earth* (Westport, CT: Greenwood Press, 1998).

"A Prayer for Rain," page 55, from the *Florentine Codex*, in Roberta H. Markman and Peter T. Markman, *The Flayed God: The Mesoamerican Mythological Tradition* (San Francisco, CA: Harper San Francisco, 1992).

"Who Are You?" page 71, from Miguel León-Portilla, *Los Antiguos Mexicanos*, in Davíd Carrasco and Eduardo Matos Moctezuma, *Moctezuma's Mexico: Visions of the Aztec World* (Niwot, CO: University Press of Colorado, 1992).

"Songs of Sorrow," page 85, from *Cantares Mexicanos*, in Miguel León-Portilla, *The Broken Spears* (Boston: Beacon Press, 1992).

INDEX

ABOUT *the* AUTHOR

VIRGINIA SCHOMP has written more than sixty titles for young readers on topics including dinosaurs, dolphins, occupations, American history, and ancient cultures. Ms. Schomp earned a Bachelor of Arts degree in English Literature from Penn State University. She lives in the Catskill Mountain region of New York with her husband, Richard, and their son, Chip.